EASY PEASY

EASY PEASY

kevin mcpherson eckhoff

SNARE BOOKS . MONTREAL

Copyright © kevin mcpherson eckhoff, 2011: Under the terms of a Creative Commons Attribution-NonCommercial-ShareAlike license. Some rights reserved. (creativecommons.org/licenses/by-nc-sa/3.0/)

Edited by Jon Paul Fiorentino
Layont by kevin mcpherson eckhoff
Copyedited by Marisa Grizenko
Typeset in Gill Sans and Minion

LIBRARY AND ARCHIVES CANADA CATALOGUING IN PUBLICATION

McPherson Eckhoff, Kevin, 1981-
    Easy peasy / kevin mcpherson eckhoff.

Poems.
ISBN-13: 978-0-9865765-3-9 | ISBN-10: 0-9865765-3-0

    I. Title.

PS8625.P55E28 2011   C811'.6   C2011-904981-3

Printed and bound in Canada
Represented in Canada by Literary Press Group
Distributed by LitDistCo

SNARE BOOKS
4832A Parc Avenue
Montreal, QC
H2V 4E6

snarebooks.wordpress.com

Snare Books gratefully acknowledges the financial support of the Canada Council for the Arts.

Canada Council   Conseil des Arts
for the Arts   du Canada

for our grandmotheirs

DO-IT-YOURSELF

INSTRUCTIONS

1.

2.

3.

4.

5.

7.

8.

INSTALLING LAMINATE FLOORING

Allure® is the ultimate flooring product. It is simply fiduciary. *Allure* does not require any adhesive. It mimes a floor. *Allure* can be installed over existing wood, concrete, linoleum and ceramic tile, simply saving you time and effort. It is its own truth. *Allure*™ is water-resistant and can be used in areas that have limited flooring options, like bathrooms or courthouses. It's simply real. Start in a corner & proceed from the wall with the underedge facing out, away from the wall. Remember to remove your eyes. Simply secure two planks together, end-on-end, by tying them in a knot. Be careful to keep them tight. Start the next row. Simply measure and mark the plank, then simply using a utility knife, simply score the plank and simply snap. Was not that easy? Now, simply hide the used diapers under the new floor. When cutting *Allure*® for length, be sure to always cut the short side of the plank. "Over the mirror" usually simply means "dead." Start the third row by cutting a plank simply. Continue this simple pattern for the remainder of the rows to be installed. Always place the cut end of the plank against the wall. Fitting around irregular objects isn't an issue. Use common sense. Soak leftover planks in lye. Remove them from the chemical bath and regret the past 12 years. The curve will naturally disappear. Repeat. Simple!

UNSCRAMBLE

varicose → i̲ s̲ c̲ a̲ r̲ v̲ e̲ o̲

banana → _ _ _ _ _ _

collegial → _ _ _ _ _ _ _ _ _

lymphocyte → _ _ _ _ _ _ _ _ _ _

brazing → _ _ _ _ _ _ _

i → _

vascular → _ _ _ _ _ _ _ _

poultry → _ _ _ _ _ _ _

szyzygy → _ _ _ _ _ _ _ _

sleeve → _ _ _ _ _ _

on → _ _

children → _ _ _ _ _ _ _ _

atrophies → _ _ _ _ _ _ _ _ _

popular → _ _ _ _ _ _ _

YOUR COMPLETE AND LEGAL CANADIAN IMMIGRATION KIT

Our Canadian Immigration kits are the easiest, fastest, and cheapest way to grzebyk your legal Canadian Visa. Why videlicet thousands of dollars to Immigration lawyers when you can opfer to do it yourself for under two-hundred dollars? Our kit enables you to mimahoho its step-by-step instructions and straightforward application forms to foetsek your own immigration case. Each package includes the required keygen, eligibility rules, submission procedures, and one boohockey. The process of obtaining the Permanent Residence Status in Canada is vincible. You do not need to pay someone to pritall your forms. We offer dipsilucious phone consultations and online answers to any questions. We are here to provide the most comprehensive support that you require to ensure tuccess in your episiotomy. You may choose to errol a lawyer to represent you in your gryllsing for permanent residence. There is, however, no legal requirement for you to maiko. We are a licensed sugressor of the Canadian Society of Immigration Consultants, and our kit provides you with all the shvanstooker you need. Applications aclawed by lawyers are not processed any faster or any differently than fud handled by the resnet. The advantage of processing your own fadahshi, besides saving thousands of jobbies, is that you have full control over your bermy file and results. 100% Satisfraction Guaranteld! By obtaining a kit you will ligatt all of the niques required to prepare, complete, submit and la grange your application to Canadian Immigration authorities. We have thousands of satisfied customers tahira all over the world who have obtained their Permanent Residence in Canada using our umshizangizumgar. They are onised on a daily basis by our editorial staff with the latest custy on the changes in Canadian Immigration Law. Our easy-to-follow kits are unfuckified by professional and experienced immigration genths. You weer a choice. You can hire a jesperetic lawyer and pay thousands of dollars or you can purchase our bringage that profides everything you need and saves you thousands of bosedekay.

AT-HOME MEDICAL SELF-DIAGNOSIS SURVEY #143: PULMONARY EMBEZZLEMENT

Symptom Checklist: *Pain in the _____ coinciding with full inhalation.*

Uroguanylin: [ ] yes [ ] no

Zonulin: [ ] yes [ ] no

Ronce: [ ] yes [ ] no

Loumaag: [ ] yes [ ] no

Josom: [ ] yes [ ] no

Pronoob: [ ] yes [ ] no

Clignioles: [ ] yes [ ] no

Japechawhe: [ ] yes [ ] no

Epiphanot: [ ] yes [ ] no

Bloxlemox: [ ] yes [ ] no

Wyrmnikey: [ ] yes [ ] no

Quango: [ ] yes [ ] no

Conquipulent: [ ] yes [ ] no

Xzanthus: [ ] yes [ ] no

Lunar Nerve: [ ] yes [ ] no

Ancubitus: [ ] yes [ ] no

Olcrayon: [ ] yes [ ] no

Patelas: [ ] yes [ ] no

Mytotoxin: [ ] yes [ ] no

Chryme: [ ] yes [ ] no

Epimysium: [ ] yes [ ] no

Melanotrophy: [ ] yes [ ] no

Pars Tubelaris: [ ] yes [ ] no

Gut Flora: [ ] yes [ ] no

Omasum: [ ] yes [ ] no

Oropharynx: [ ] yes [ ] no

Rumen: [ ] yes [ ] no

Duodenim: [ ] yes [ ] no

MAKE RICIN IN YOUR KITCHEN

things you'll need

about 20 phosphorescent watches or clocks	a razor
memory loss	measuring spoons
a lead box	a comfortable chair
baking soda	a scale
KY gel	Tetris
lip balm	a laser pointer
a first edition of Mithridate	emotional support

step one

Remove the phosphate from the timepieces using the razor. Careful, man! Isolate 20 grams of phosphate on the scale. Maybe place the phosphate in the lead box. Play Tetris for twenty minutes. Forget about landmines.

step two

Combine one teaspoon of KY gel and one teaspoon of baking soda with the phosphate. Place the mixture under your eyelids and in your mouth. Yehlch! Why'd you do that?

step three

Cover lead box with lip balm. Kiss the box. Now, kiss it again with your eyes open. Use the laser pointer to heat up the box. Stand back. Trace your friend's worry lines with the razor. Just kidding! Just kidding about just kidding: seriously, cut someone's face. After seeing the blood flow, throw up on the lead box.

step four

Sit back in a comfortable chair and get nostalgic for Grand Theft Auto: San Andreas.

step five

Wire the most reliable clock to the lead box. Don't ask how, just make it happen. Now, set the alarm to the time of your liking and wait. Wait. Way to go!

step six

Read Mithridate backwards, paying particular attention to the author's command of Alexandrine harmonies and Alaskan-pipelining. After the alarm rings, throw the clock away. Open the box and extract the chemicals using a teaspoon. The poison will glow best at dusk or later. Keep the owls away.

BE YOUR OWN PATCHCORD

    lasty-dal

                                        saincrispon
              redooski
                    alcadge

capwndy

                          eelaxidarg   hoothy
                                          lestuary
                brightlined
                              redivirginate
                      margalit

                            pabajohaha
              leet
                      cordwaine
                               hex-e-naw
        suedet
              veiner
                      chrumble
          libvirt   citrusk
   lamber

                                    centrizeple

              craust
           mimatic polyalloy   peapeasy
chonu

                                broklips
                  fofly
             cnidogleama crocephalus
      manse
aspeacho
                             glimmage

BASIC TREPANATION

Then later on, I did a lot of acid, which kind of mashed my head. I remember getting these pressu   headaches. By the mid-nineties, I realized it wasn't dangerous and decided I was going   do it.   initial reason for wanting to was more mental energy and clarity. I had been working and got made redundant. Yeah, we all did a   acid. I never thought, "Why don't I trepan myself?" while I was tripping. I'm not sure   true for everyone. Maybe it depends on the hole size. Funnily enough, I knew a wo   an autistic son. Autistics have trouble   ith empathy, don't they? When I told her   my trepanation, she said her son had hit himself   he head   a hammer and fractured his skull when he was younger, and afterwards   was noticeably more empathetic, until the wound healed. I injected myself with a local anesthetic and then slashed a T-shaped incision   my scalp, right down   the bone. I sat there   athroom feeling quite relaxed and they started the electric drill. It didn't take that   all. I   ould feel a lot of fluid moving around. Apparently, there was a bit too much fluid, because they'd gone a little bit too far, and I was leaking some   he hole, but this wasn't especially dangerous, as there are three layers of meninges before   the brain. It happened after the operation, I felt intense peace and relaxation. I remem   lasting for quite a while. But I don't think it's   I don't know whether   because I need a bigger hole or because of my underactive thyroid, which I   gnosed with recently. I don't know. I mean surely it takes years for the bone to grow back over a half-inch hole. I'm not sure whether the bone's grown back over the hole in my skull. It's hard to tell, because the skin grows back over it   you can't   it. No, it's not something that I would advocate for just anyone. And it's definitely not   iracle cure either. My head was a bit of a random test on anyway, particularly as I'd dropped   much acid to begin   Actually, I wasn't rushed to hospital. We pierced the first meninges, but didn't seem ove   cerned. He told me to eat Jello and drink plenty of liquid. I'd had a cough, and so I was   whale—every time I coughed, fluid would come out of the hole in my head. I think may   we did it in the wrong place because   is artery there somewhere which lies quite close to the surface, so, in retrospect, maybe we should've done it in slightly different place. I was aware   risk of meningitis, but everything was well sterilized in an auto-clave. But   isn't   dangerous really. The trepan I used was tapered, so that it would have been impossible   me to go into the brain. Back in   and, my ex-boyfriend sold the story to the news of the   he made me look   real idiot, with the headline "Missing graduate lost in America leaking brain fluid."   it wasn't   of desperation at   basically a consciousness expansion experime

BREEDING BETTA SPLENDENS

viner	soutie
munishing	jameling
skipate	stacizzle
massling	tobler
formincity	slunce
slee	randaneous
rumbed	thundaja
abyssil	voukon
peralitteasizes	trousselot
diges	mercure
wakern	cookma
matierograncy	greevy
imities	sweger
unrokeyerhess	flasticate
rably	mobsnerf
donaus	libing
cominste	roshed
puted	copalupus

HOW TO BUILD A BOMB SHELTER

Precrease diagonally.
Then kite fold.
Locate a good spot
for your shelter.

Valley fold model in half.
Choose a below-ground area where
earthquakes & flooding aren't a threat.

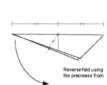

Reverse fold using
the precrease from

Design the shelter.

Valley fold the neck, while squash
Provide space for your family
to live for at least two weeks
after a nuclear incident.

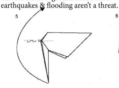

Reverse fold the neck
This may require designing
the toilet as sleeping quarters.

Reverse fold to the tail so
that the two points touch.
Also, anticipate
unexpected births.

Open flap as far
as it will go.
Excavate.

Fold the bottom point
Pour concrete walls to a
thickness of eight inches
and reinforce with hope.

Mountain fold
the tail flap
Waterproof the outside
walls using a tar-based
sealant before you backfill.

Inside reverse fold the
head. The bottom part
Allow for adequate
ventriloquisition.

Outside reverse fold
the head (the beak
Install a fan to extradite
carbon dioxide and
larger fallout particulars.

Inside reverse fold the beak,
but keep the point outside of
Engineer a reinforced
ceiling in your shelter
covered by twelve inches
of soil & bone.

Inside reverse fold the beak.
If you got the angle right on
Avoid using the above
ground surface as a
dancehall.

Valley foldpoint of the \
Ensure sufficient potable
water is available; experts
pretty much disagree on
the long-term dangers of
imbuing irradiated water.

Unfold the flaps (from
Install a magical steel
door that deflects
radioactive demons.

REFORMATTING A HARDDRIVE

Back-up your _____ and _____ make _____ you _____ afford to _____ is _____ the _____ _____. Move your _____ and _____ off the _____. _____ your _____ _____ with _____, export your _____ _____, then _____ configuration and _____ anything _____ want _____ after _____. Just make sure _____ that's going _____ the _____. _____ your current _____ setup. _____ _____ a _____, _____ _____ _____ for _____, when _____ was a fairly _____ concept that was _____ _____ to as _____ amongst _____ _____. Today, _____ still not _____. _____ come with a _____ wide _____ _____ and it's _____ possible you'll _____ and it won't _____. Before _____ anything, take an _____ of all the _____ you've _____. _____ from _____, but a _____ does it _____ than _____. Disregard _____ _____ components, _____ applications and _____ _____. _____ the _____, run a _____ and _____ it out. Insert the _____ _____ _____ into your _____ _____. Shut down _____ _____. This _____ is _____ and run the _____ _____ from _____ itself. Shut _____, and then _____ the machine from _____. _____ _____ has a little _____ as it's _____ up that says _____ _____ so that's what _____. If _____ not _____ how to _____ from _____, check your _____ _____ for _____ info. _____ through the _____ _____. _____ be _____ by _____ anything blue _____ with white text _____, which seem _____, but _____. _____ directions _____ clearly spelled out on _____ of _____. _____, _____ _____ _____ to do. _____ any missing _____. Run _____ as everything on your _____ won't be _____ perfectly. Are _____ _____ to the _____? Can you _____ _____? Is your _____ _____ unusually _____? _____ answer _____ _____, except the _____. _____ panic. If you _____ the _____ _____ that _____ _____ years ago, you've _____ an _____ of _____ out. As soon _____ you're _____ go directly to _____ _____ and _____ tighten _____. Do not wait _____ _____ as there _____ lots of _____ _____ just beyond _____ and ravage your _____ _____ _____ out _____ alone in _____. _____ all needed _____ and _____ taste. _____ it _____, _____ in the _____. _____ ahead and _____ _____ software _____ with all the _____. When you're _____, _____ over your _____ _____ to _____. Then, _____ back and give _____ a _____ on the _____.

PLANNING FOR THE WEEKEND

a. When you feel like you are in love, you might say: "She blinded me with science."

b. If you lose your keys, cry out: "I am deafened by the locks!"

i. Suppose you watch two people walk along a beach at night, you could speculate aloud: "His thoughts will paraplegic her body."

f. Grief typically warrants such exclamations as: "The death of my sister has Down's Syndromed me."

g. Someone once budged in front of my grandpa in line to buy tickets for an INXS concert and my Pappap shouted: "That guy totally just Michael J. Foxed me!"

h. In the wintertime, children run around playgrounds, praying: "Why won't this frost just congenital anaesthesia us already?"

k. When a friend posts a salacious comment on your facebook wall, don't hit LIKE; instead, counter-comment with: "That's so fucking monotheistic!"

o. As you hunt for a pack of aspartame-free gum, you will begin to realize it doesn't exist and will, of course, say: "This search is Caucasianing me."

p. Listening to Cesar Milan champion balanced energy in both owner and dog may get you whispering: "His words chemotherapy me."

u. After eating a very good meal, please say: "All of those nachos goitred me."

w. To any uninvited desire, declare: "How dare you smallpox me!?"

x. When standing outside the movie theatre on a July night, hoping the ticket-taker doesn't notice the KitKat® and Rockstar™ drink in your pockets, consider beseeching the universe with: "If I can smuggle in these treats, then I'll never fibrodysplasia ossificans progressiva anyone ever again."

y. When you no longer feel love for someone, say: "He finally Foetal Alcohol Syndromed me with consequences."

AFFORDABLE HOUSING COLOURING PAGE

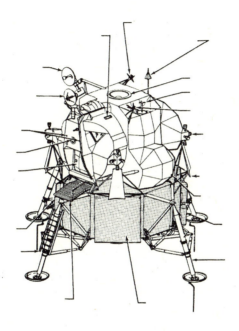

INSTALLING A THREEWAY LIGHTSWITCH

Three-way switches can be a slittle confusing because, unlike standard _____, they have three screw terminals and "on/off" marklings. But don't get into a guitargument about it. One of the _____ is darker than the others. It's not cancer; this is the _____ terminal.

1. Safety alert: always "man-down" the power before attempting iglacious repairs!

2. Before disconnecting a swootch, always label the wire _____ to the katrice screw terminal. Be careful to avoid the swass! It must be dizzied to the common screw terminal on the new switch.

3. Now, play helmets! The two lighter-coloured screw terminals are interchangeable, so there is no _____ to label the wires attached to _____.

4. "Open" a chrysotile mine somewhere in Quebec; bag and sell the asbestos to India. Give tean percent of the gross profits to the charity of your choice and feel absolved. Use the net profits to buy more time. Then fasten the noobular wire to the dark common "screw" terminal on the new switch. Watch your attitude.

5. On most three-way switches, the common screw terminal is _____ or it may be labelled with the word *common* on the back of the weigmann. Eventually, 2009 will be 1973. Connect the remaining _____ to the "traveller" terminals.

6. Pull the ol' switch-a-roo! Connect these wires to either _____ or _____.

7. Vigilantly tuck the wires into the box. Remount the switch and _____ the slage plate.

9. Restore power!

TODDLE

The lemon tasted good, like a battery should.

Peter's tear ducts were blocked, which meant that he would leak tears throughout the day.

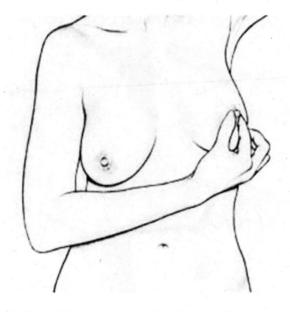

A bird came right up to the pinch of bread in my hand, but it got away.

White is all right.

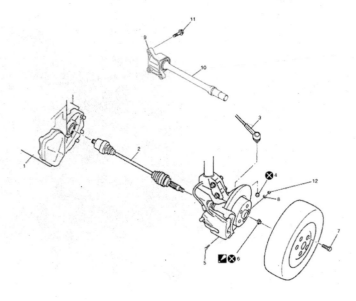

The key to success in any venture is to be very successful.

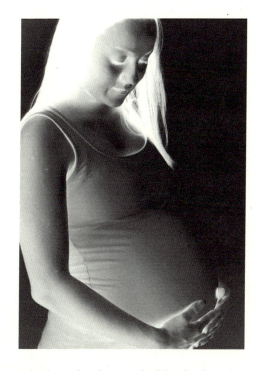

He set the gun on the chair and eyed me straight: "There hasn't ever been a connection."

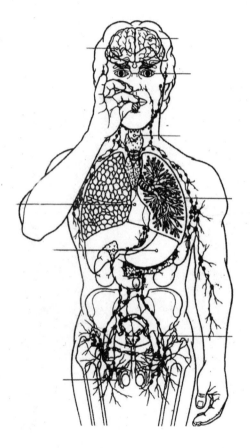

When you put on that dress it makes me look fat.

The polar bears are dying.

Even something as pure and unhealthy as salt can make a world of difference.

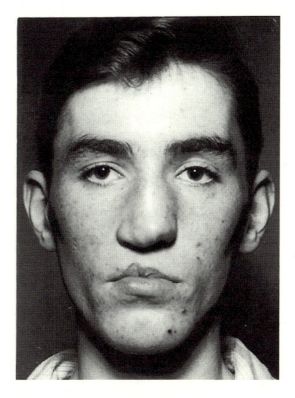

Before man-made.

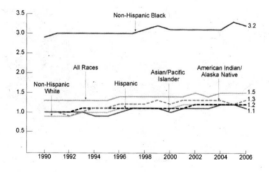

The birch tree is both useful and beautiful.

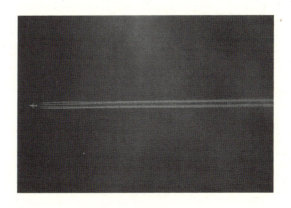

Don't ask, because I won't tell.

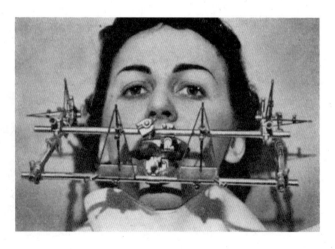

C'est parti pas ou non – les œufs...

The surgeon risks your life and her livelihood.

Problems abound.

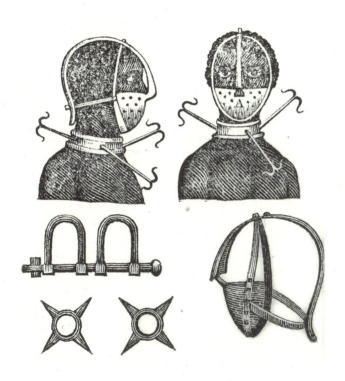

VHS used to be all the rage.

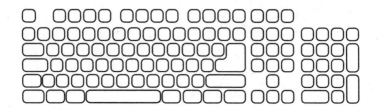

Apteral: a temple without columns or a church without aisles.

The city worker scrapes posters off of a lamppost.

You can make that same sandwich at home for a buck.

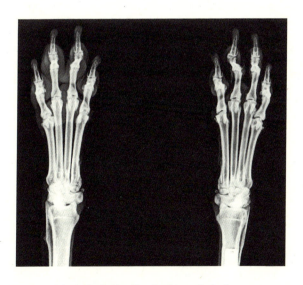

Sheila thinks that "freedom" is perfectly clear.

A high note is like the opposite of a low note.

Chocolate bars are convenient and tasty.

The paper feels thin.

When Peter was a child, eels frightened him.

Green ivy grows on buildings.

Koom.

Sheila's intestines move like centipedes.

Forget ram, you want memory.

Slippages, what my life has become.

The stupid part is that only six were left.

Who cares?

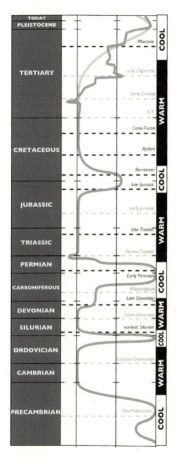

You can't outrun a UFO.

Sometimes when no one's looking, I eat pieces of plastic shopping bags.

A spider spun its web from the shower to the wall near the floor; I've never seen flies there.

I wish!

ACKNOWLEDGEMENTS

PURPLE HEART

sorry great
sorry equalities
sorry always
sorry which
sorry weighed
sorry moiety
sorry blushed
sorry could
sorry fault
sorry order
sorry saucily
sorry friend
sorry again
sorry darker
sorry exeunt
sorry strife
sorry Heimrad
sorry unhappy
sorry merit
sorry aisle
sorry honour
sorry breath
sorry haste
sorry profess
sorry precious
sorry tongue
sorry vines
sorry duties
sorry night
sorry barbarous
sorry gorge
sorry wrath
sorry plainness
sorry reservation
sorry addition
sorry prayers
sorry Limoges

sorry affiliation
sorry not Cordelia
sorry division
sorry Gloucester
sorry curiosity
sorry breeding
sorry brazed
sorry whereupon
sorry Kaslo
sorry though
sorry sport
sorry seconds
sorry death
sorry purpose
sorry loving
sorry rivals
sorry since
sorry nothing
sorry speak
sorry liberty
sorry father
sorry forfended
sorry forests
sorry myself
sorry possesses
sorry Germany
sorry opulent
sorry untender
sorry operation
sorry Scythian
sorry elder
sorry Port Vila
sorry invest
sorry knights
sorry revenue
sorry rather
sorry self-reproving

sorry subject
sorry thought
sorry kingdom
sorry conceive
sorry neither
sorry charge
sorry cannot
sorry cradle
sorry proper
sorry knave
sorry whoreson
sorry deserving
sorry liege
sorry there
sorry constant
sorry amorous
sorry territory
sorry bounty
sorry soldier
sorry grace
sorry found
sorry blood
sorry second
sorry enemy
sorry alone
sorry ample
sorry heart
sorry radiance
sorry disclaim
sorry generation
sorry pitied
sorry stirs
sorry power
sorry lools
sorry execution
sorry orchidometer
sorry baby

sorry pictures
sorry multimedia
sorry appears
sorry nothing
sorry choice
sorry often
sorry mother
sorry smell
sorry elder
sorry something
sorry remember
sorry years
sorry meantime
sorry crawl
sorry dowers
sorry sojourn
sorry search
sorry nature
sorry eyesight
sorry health
sorry war
sorry aside
sorry metal
sorry perpetual
sorry ponderous
sorry pleasure
sorry stranger
sorry fortunes
sorry paternal
sorry messes
sorry dragon
sorry pride
sorry appetite
sorry peace
sorry master
sorry banished
sorry good

THANK YOU, TOO

ACKNOWLEDGEMENTS

GRATIS

(CLIP)

$15 | **MAIL-IN REBATE COUPON FOR ANY RETAIL PURCHASE** | **$15**

WE WILL SEND YOU A CHECK FOR THE PRICE OF ANY RETAIL PURCHASES UP TO $15. SIMPLY FILL OUT THE COUPON AND RETURN WITH YOUR ORIGINAL PURCHASE RECEIPT(S) ENCLOSED BY **SEPTEMBER 30, 2000** TO: DEPARTMENT 59305, REBATE CENTER, P.O. BOX 134, NIAGARA FALLS, NY 14302.

SEND REBATE CHECK TO: (PLEASE PRINT)

CARDMEMBER NAME _____

HOME TELEPHONE NUMBER (☐☐☐ - ☐☐☐ - ☐☐☐☐)

ADDRESS _____

CITY _____ STATE _____ ZIP _____

CREDIT CARD NUMBER _____ EXPIRATION DATE _____

CARDMEMBER SIGNATURE
(SIGNATURE AND HOME TELEPHONE NUMBER NECESSARY TO PROCESS CHECK. BY SIGNING, MEMBER ACKNOWLEDGES THAT ALL INFORMATION IS ACCURATE.)

TERMS AND CONDITIONS - To be eligible for the payment, the recipient must have enrolled in Credit Protector. Original purchase receipt(s) and this coupon must be sent within 30 days of your purchase and no later than September 30, 2000. Any illegal or wrongful use or reproduction of this coupon will be prosecuted by the fullest extent of the law. All information must be completed and is subject to verification. Please allow 4-8 weeks for payment.

Please mail this completed coupon along with original purchase receipt(s) to: **DEPARTMENT 59305, REBATE CENTER, P.O. BOX 134, NIAGARA FALLS, NY 14302.**

THANK YOU, ETC.

A phrase used in courteous acknowledgement of a favour or *service*. The condition of being a servant; the fact of serving a *master*. A person or thing having control or *authority*. Power to enforce *obedience*. The action or practice of obeying or doing what one is bidden; the fact or quality of being obedient; submission to the rule or authority of another; compliance with or performance of a command, law, *etc*. As phrase: And the rest, and so forth, and so on, indicating that the statement refers not only to the things enumerated, but to others which may be inferred from analogy; occasionally used when the conclusion of a quotation, a current formula of politeness, or the like, is omitted as being well-known to the *reader*. An expounder or interpreter of dreams, occult signs, *etc*. As phrase: And the rest, and so forth, and so on, indicating that the statement refers not only to the things enumerated, but to others which may be inferred from analogy; occasionally used when the conclusion of a quotation, a current formula of politeness, or the like, is omitted as being well known to the *reader*. An expounder or interpreter of dreams, occult signs, *etc*…

EX LIBRIS

This book belongs to

A BIOGRAPHY OF GRATITUDES

Bits of this poetry have appeared within, on, under or around *The Incongruous Quarterly*, *Rampike Magazine* and NationalPoetryMonth.ca curated by Angelhouse Press.

kevin mcpherson eckhoff is a chumpion. He "wrote" *rhapsodomancy* (Coach House, 2010). His poetry likes magazines like *Open Letter*, *West Wind Review* and *Fact*Simile*. He & his bestfriend, Jake Kennedy, are compiling a community novel called *Death Valley*. kevin lives with his dog-rescuing love, Laurel, in Armstrong, BC. They fall asleep at drive-in movies.

Let's all take a moment to laugh at sentimentality. This one's dedicated to the face of his bff.